Nidaros Jazz Mass

Bob Chilcott

for SSAA, piano, and optional bass and drum kit

Vocal score

MUSIC DEPARTMENT

OXFORD
UNIVERSITY PRESS

OXFORD
UNIVERSITY PRESS

Great Clarendon Street, Oxford OX2 6DP,
United Kingdom

Oxford University Press is a department of the University of Oxford.
It furthers the University's objective of excellence in research, scholarship,
and education by publishing worldwide. Oxford is a registered trade mark of
Oxford University Press in the UK and in certain other countries

© Oxford University Press 2012

First published 2012

Impression: 8

ISBN 978-0-19-338633-4

Music origination by Enigma Music Production Services, Amersham, Bucks.
Printed in Great Britain on acid-free paper by
Halstan & Co. Ltd, Amersham, Bucks.

Contents

Composer's note

Nidaros Jazz Mass is the second shortened Mass setting that I have written for upper voices and jazz combo. It was first performed on 3 June 2012 by its dedicatees, the Nidaros Cathedral Girls' Choir, in the eleventh-century gothic cathedral in Trondheim, Norway.

Jazz has always played an important part in my life as a composer, arranger, and singer. During my time as a tenor in the King's Singers I performed and made an album with the legendary jazz pianist George Shearing. George, who died early in 2011, was a remarkable musician who had a huge impact on me, as he inevitably did on any other musician who was lucky enough to come into contact with him. He was very much on my mind when I began to write this piece shortly after he died.

The *Nidaros Jazz Mass* can be performed as it stands by voices and piano, with the piano part played as written. I would, however, urge the pianist to improvise freely on the chord structure, and I would encourage the addition of bass and drums, and perhaps guitar and extra percussion, to the ensemble. An annotated bass part is available separately for this purpose, and I am grateful to the jazz pianist Alexander Hawkins for his help in the preparation of this part.

Duration: *c.*15 minutes

Also available:
Nidaros Jazz Mass Bass, Drum Kit, and optional Guitar Part (ISBN 978-0-19-338669-3)

Commissioned by Nidaros Cathedral Girls' Choir and conductor Anita Brevik
for their 20th anniversary

Nidaros Jazz Mass

BOB CHILCOTT

1. Kyrie

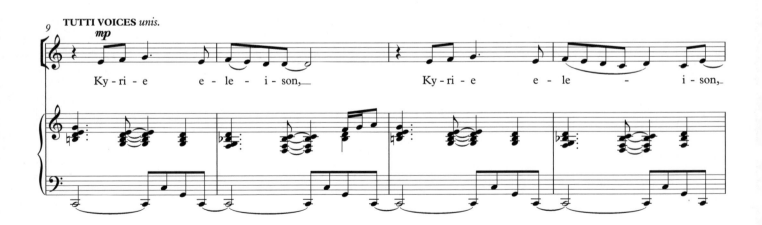

*The piano part can be played as written or used as a guide. Bass and drum kit can join *ad lib.*

Printed in Great Britain

OXFORD UNIVERSITY PRESS, MUSIC DEPARTMENT, GREAT CLARENDON STREET, OXFORD OX2 6DP
The Moral Rights of the Composer have been asserted. Photocopying this copyright material is ILLEGAL.

e - le - i - son, e - le - i - son,

e - le - i - son, e - le - i - son,

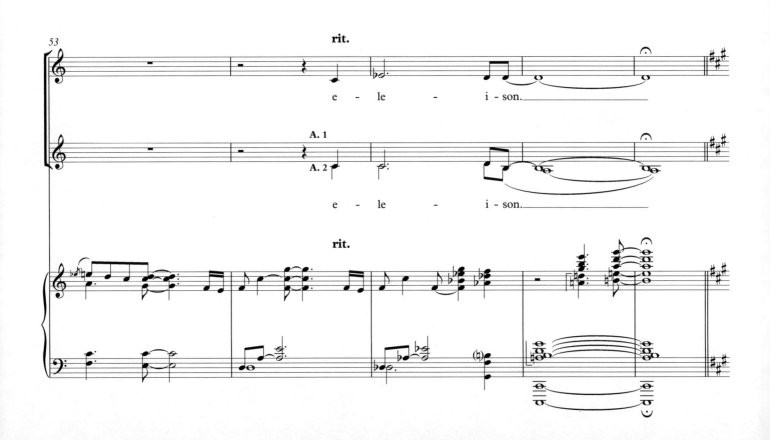

e - le - i - son.

e - le - i - son.

2. Gloria

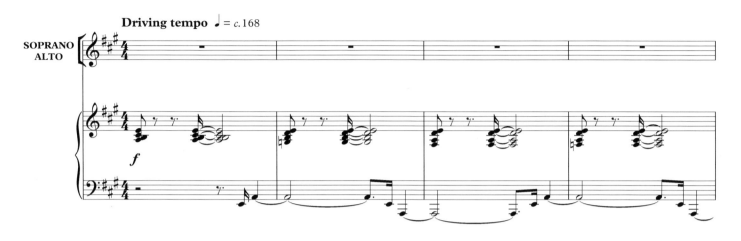

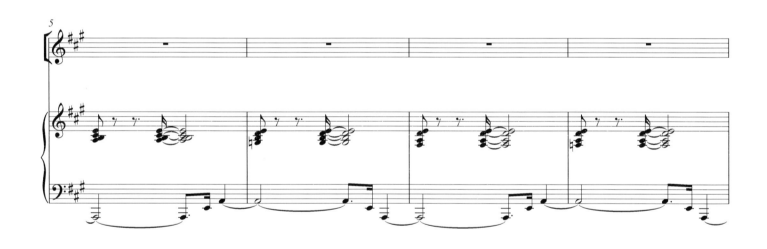

Glo - ri - a in ex - cel - sis De - o, in ex - cel - sis De - o, glo - ri - a!

Gloria in excelsis Deo, in excelsis Deo, gloria!

Gloria in excelsis Deo, in excelsis Deo, gloria!

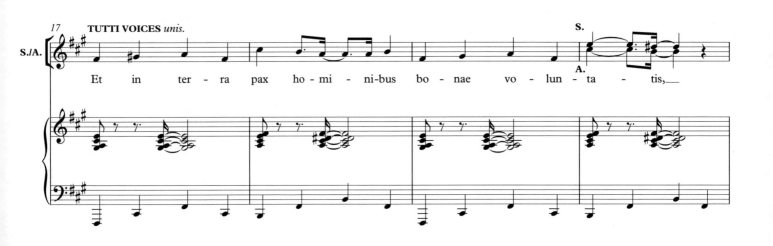

TUTTI VOICES *unis.*

Et in terra pax hominibus bonae voluntatis,

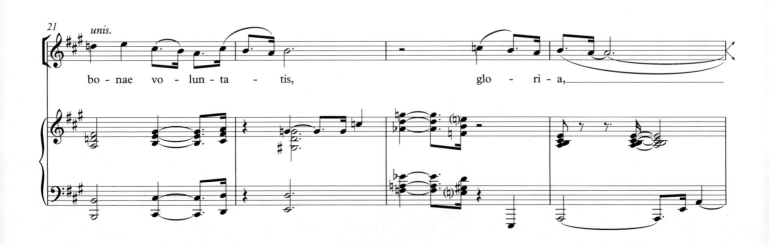

unis.

bonae voluntatis, gloria,

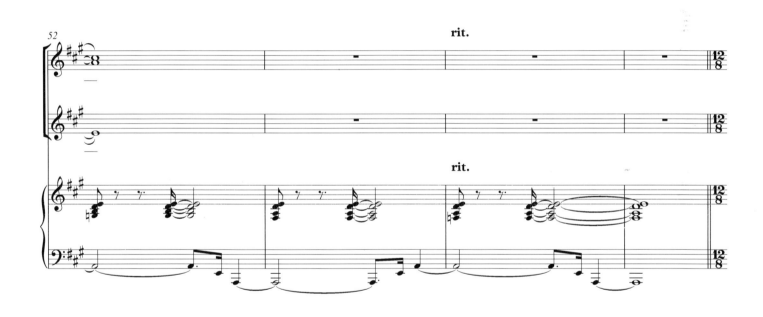

Rex cae-les - tis,___ De-us Pa-ter om-ni ___ - po - tens,___ om-ni-po-tens.___

S. Do - mi - ne Fi - li___ u - ni - ge - ni - te, Je - su

A. Do - mi - ne Fi - li___ u - ni - ge - ni - te, Je - su Chris - te.___

Chris - te. Do - mi - ne De - us, A - gnus De - i, Fi - li - us Pa - tris,___ Qui

___ Do - mi - ne De - us, A - gnus De - i, Fi - li - us Pa - tris,

no - bis, mi - se - re - re, mi - se - re - re no - bis.

no - bis, mi - se - re - re, mi - se - re - re no - bis.

Tempo primo ♩ = c.168

Tempo primo ♩ = c.168

f

TUTTI VOICES *unis.*

f

S./A.

Quo - ni - am tu so - lus san - ctus, tu so - lus san - ctus, quo - ni - am,

3. Sanctus

4. Benedictus

5. Agnus Dei

Processed in England by Enigma Music Production Services, Amersham, Bucks.
Printed in England by Halstan & Co. Ltd, Amersham, Bucks.